Wintering tundra swans, Tule Lake National Wildlife Refuge, California.

Wintering mallard pair, Eau Claire River, Wisconsin.

Wood duck pair on loafing spot near nest, St. Louis Bay, Wisconsin.

Wintering lesser snow geese, Bosque del Apache National Wildlife Refuge, New Mexico.

Published by Thomasson-Grant, Inc.:
Frank L. Thomasson III and John F. Grant, Directors;
C. Douglas Elliott, Product Development;
Megan R. Youngquist, Art Director;
Carolyn M. Clark, Senior Editor;
Jim Gibson, Production Manager.
Designed by Megan R. Youngquist
Text by Owen Andrews
Introduction by H. Albert Hochbaum
Technical advising by Jerome R. Serie
Copyright © 1988 by Thomasson-Grant, Inc. All rights reserved.
Photographs copyright © 1988 as credited on page 135.
This book, or any portions thereof, may not be reproduced in any
form without written permission of the publisher, Thomasson-Grant, Inc.
Library of Congress Catalog Card Number: 87-51381
ISBN 0-934738-37-8
Printed in the United States by Hoechstetter Printing, Inc.
95 94 93 92 91 90 89 88   5 4 3 2 1

Any inquiries should be directed to Thomasson-Grant, Inc.,
One Morton Drive, Suite 500, Charlottesville, Virginia 22901,
telephone (804) 977-1780.

THOMASSON·GRANT

WATERFOWL OF NORTH AMERICA

Introduction By H. Albert Hochbaum

Pintail waiting for his mate, Charles Mix County, South Dakota.

heir voices come to us at daybreak. Off and on we hear them through the morning, then watch their dark lines moving against the sunset's glow. Farmers, stockbrokers, store clerks, each of us sometime, somewhere, stops to listen. There are little schools in the way beyond where the teacher lets her children out to call and wave at the first spring flocks. In a hospital, someone turns to the window and for the moment loses fear. To the south, the high flyers bark out their farewells: *until October, goodbye.* In the far north, tent flaps open to the south wind and the calls of renewal. Across the length and breadth of North America wild geese announce the arrival of spring, reminding all human beings of their ties to wild things, wild places.

The geese are talking to one another. Each is saying to its companions, *Here I am...where are you? Here I am...where are you?* Aloft in storm and cloud, the voices hold the flock together. They speak out loudly against wind and distance so that others of their kind, strayed or lost, may know the way. Under fair sky the calls continue for reassurance and to reassure. *Come along, do not tire. We are on the right course and will soon stop for rest.* It is no fable, but a truth of nature; experienced elders lead the way.

Like the baying of hounds on chase, the flock call heard from afar is a blend of sound, but every bird is talking. Mothers and fathers know the voices of their families; brothers and sisters recognize each other. They fly boldly onward, even the youngest worldly in ways we can never comprehend, strong and free within the mass of air, at home in the sky, with the sun and the clouds, the moon and the stars. Their flight talk is the language of togetherness, as important to migrating geese as drums and marching songs are to soldiers. We groundlings are stirred by their passing, awed by their travels.

We all have an innate awareness of nature's primitive beauties: mountains and valleys, rivers and streams, lakes and oceans, fair-weather clouds and massed thunderheads, and the patterns that wildfowl create against these backdrops: tundra swans in their majesty, dashing bands of blue-winged teal, darts of gadwall and green-winged teal, long, wavering lines of canvasback and redhead, mallards and pintails 100,000 strong.

The sound of their wings as they pass is like wind rushing through poplars. Always, always, the Canada geese, large and small in their several races. And the wavies, the lesser snow geese, mass in spring passage, two, three, sometimes five thousand in one web of lines, dipping, wavering, holding together. Bright chevrons cross and blend, lose shape and recover, rise and fall to reveal the shape of the wind. Again and again little family groups shift from one part of the flock to another. Their voices join in a chorus that hurries people to windows and doorsteps, charmed for a few moments, moved by the very same sounds that fell to earth ten million years before man evolved.

They begin their return in autumn. On the western shore of Hudson Bay, some little wavies start their migration southward only a few hours after they have made their first flights. The parents lead them low above the golden shoreline, stopping often for rest and food, taking the long way around the bay until the young are strong enough for the southerly passage. Some of the little Canada geese bred in the high Arctic still have natal down on their heads and necks, and baby voices, the *weeps, weeps* of hatchlings, when they reach North Dakota in September. Alighting after a long flight, they quickly fall asleep before they eat. Tundra swans shepherd their gray cygnets, two, three, rarely four squealing young with each mother and father. Yearlings, now with adult voices and plumage, make up part of the southbound flocks. When one is injured, crippled, and left behind, a family tragedy of any autumn, there comes the plaintive swan song, *Wait! Here I am, where are you? Wait!*

In autumn the many species of ducks forgather on lakes and marshes. Each bird is an individual within the society of these aggregations. There are friends and strangers in the multitudes, but no family ties. Among all ducks, a massive separation of the sexes occurs in May or June. Every hen has brought her drake north to the home marsh where he waited close by while she laid her clutch. Then, sometime after she has started to incubate, almost always before the young are hatched, he abandons her to rear her young alone. Off he goes, sometimes several hundred miles away, to pass the summer molt with thousands of other males. Now on the fall staging areas, and still later on the wintering waters, there is a rejoining, a reshuffling of birds until drakes and hens flock together. Juveniles who have explored far and wide ever since they were fledged join the autumn society. Beginning now, in the annual cycle of renewal, a mate must be found, courted, and won. October is not too early to begin.

Stand some autumn evening on the Chesapeake's eastern shore. The tide flows softly in, whispering a gentle song offered by no other salt water in the world. Anyone cupping his ear might hear a distant rippling as of water running over shoals: canvasback feeding. Listen carefully. Hear the hiccupping and cooing of courting drakes. Some hen has let them know that more than food is on her mind. At dusk, as through the day, she is searching for an attractive male—not just any bird, but the strongest, most aggressive bull-necked drake, with a sheen to his brick-red head and a sparkle of good health in his vermilion eye. She needs an experienced individual, the kind of mate who will protect her in her faraway nesting marsh.

Over where the creek enters the Bay, a black duck hen sings out her loud hail call, a decrescendo of quacks that blatantly entices. *Swish*, two black duck males drop down to the creek mouth only to find half a dozen other suitors. There is plenty of time, and that little hen is going to play the field.

At Henry, Illinois, as elsewhere up and down the Illinois River, over the breadth of the Mississippi Valley, and in marshlands west to California, mallard hens are calling in the same voice as their dark eastern relatives.

On the rice fields of the Sacramento Valley, migrating pintails suddenly turn to their species' courting sound, a bright little whistle from the shallows. Redhead drakes are mewing before interested females on the Laguna Madre along the Texas coast. It is not yet December. The wildfowl have been at their wintering quarters hardly a month, yet hormonal changes have made these birds sexual beings once again.

The calls of courting waterfowl are also vital to the two and a half million North Americans who, for all the trappings of our modern lives, still bend to the innate hunting urge. Some hunters, following ancient traditions, learn to talk like ducks. With a walnut and reed instrument, men hail-call passing flocks of mallards or black ducks. When the birds tip their wings, they are offered further sexual enticements, irresistible if skillfully rendered. On California rice fields, pintails are lured to join wooden decoys by men piping on flutelike whistles. At the edge of open water, lesser scaup bend to decoys on hearing the hunter's trilled purring. Canvasback and redhead turn to imitations of the female's growl. For wild geese, there need be no sexual overtones. The hunter simply yodels in his best wildfowling voice, *Here we are, here we are, rest and peace, food and companionship.*

Open water, good food, and part-time security from gunfire are what Canada geese seek when they winter at places like the South Platte River of Colorado and downtown Rochester, Minnesota. In all of these gatherings, social structure is founded on the family. Mother and father share a lifelong partnership, spending the seasons together, seldom more than a few yards apart. Unlike human beings, all geese hold to double parenting. Single-parent families occur only when tragedy strikes one mate or the other. The high rearing success of geese probably relates to their faithfulness to each other and to their young. In the spring the gander stands faithful guard while his mate incubates her eggs. Through the summer she is always on one side of the brood, he on the other. In autumn the family goes south, one parent leading, the other bringing up the rear.

In early autumn the youngsters are shy, clinging to mother and father who defend a small family circle within the crowd. As autumn settles into winter, the young begin to reach out socially, always in the context of the family. Brothers and sisters become acquainted with first cousins, second cousins, and cousins many times removed. They meet and learn to avoid aunts, uncles, grandparents, great-grandparents—some great by a power beyond measure, for wild geese are capable of reproducing into their 40th year. The society is further complicated by yearlings hatched in the spring of the previous year. They are experienced but not yet mature, serving somewhat as buffers between the callow goslings and all adults.

At first the goslings make only tentative moves outward. They approach with heads high, cautiously alert, ready to turn back quickly to the family. There are hissed threats, meetings with heads low, necks outstretched or bent. There are bold advances, hasty retreats, friendly responses, many harsh rejections, some bitter fights. In all of this, goslings of dominant parents

are the most venturesome, large families the boldest. When a young gander from a strong family sneaks up behind another youngster to bill-poke it in the rear, the latter jumps forward with spread wings and a startled *squank.* It is quite another story when a young bird so pokes a yearling, who, after initial surprise, turns upon him viciously. The offender seeks family refuge; father quickly comes to the rescue and a wing-striking, feather-pulling fight ensues. Victorious, father runs to mother; the two call out loudly and advertise their strength and togetherness with their triumph ceremony, necks upstretched, heads rolling.

Feeling its way out from the family, a youngster joins with a member of the opposite sex, sometimes one its own age. The two feed, rest, and walk side by side, the gander challenging others of his age. They wander about on their own, but not far from her family or his. Each may discover a more interesting companion; often a young female joins with an older gander. Or, as the season advances, the young goose and gander may face each other on water, chest to chest, their heads dipping rhythmically in the precopulatory ritual of all geese. Although neither is sexually mature, the young gander may mount the young goose.

In winter, many of the two-year-olds form firm pair relationships, the beginning of their lifetime together. When they move through the crowd, younger geese step aside in deference, while they themselves carefully avoid confrontation with their elders. If there is any shred of an excuse, the two join in a full-blown triumph ceremony.

In all this mix there are brothers and sisters hatched 15 or 20 years apart, great-great-aunts, uncles beyond counting, grandparents, together with just plain friends of the family in their many generations. Here is a genealogical confusion no scientist could ever sort out with colored neck markings and numbered leg bands, but the geese know where they stand in this complex society. Every goose has some distinguishing characteristic by which it is known to its associates, not for just

an autumn or a winter, but for a lifetime.

When geese join us in our communities, they quickly come to know individuals and to distinguish friend from foe. Twenty or thirty geese are friends with the elderly lady who brings crusts every afternoon at four. At ten minutes to four they await her at the appointed place. They lift their heads when they see her coming far across the lawn. The generous woman in Rochester, the kindly man in Boston, the unruly boys in Denver are recognized in any clothing. It is the individual human being these birds learn to know, regardless of what he or she wears on a given day. Truly, it must be the character itself that is probed, understood, accepted. When the lady brings a friend, the birds are standoffish, wary for the moment until an understanding is established.

Throughout their lives, waterfowl consider the world about them, pass judgments, make decisions, sometimes make mistakes. Their world is our world. We are their companions, their adversaries, competitors steadily taking for ourselves their land and water. For some, we have become their benefactors, protecting, culturing certain populations. We saved the greater

snow goose and the giant Canada goose when they were on the brink of extinction. Inspired to poetry by their "dark rune against the sunset glow," we find them relaxing to watch as they feed and loaf and court near our homes. We travel thousands of miles and spend several billion dollars each year to hunt, bag, and bring them to our dinner tables.

Tall reeds, the plumed queen of the prairies, glow under the October sun, golden marsh as far as one can see east and west. Several miles to the south, dark blocks of oak and maple mark the edge of farmland. To the north, a long, narrow ridge of trees follows the southern shoreline of Lake Manitoba. Between lakeshore and farmland, the reeds open to a wide reach of water, ultramarine as only in midautumn. Elsewhere in the 50 square miles of the Delta Marsh, reed beds enclose other connecting waters, large and small, hidden sloughs and winding creeks, all establishing the pattern of one of the world's great waterfowl gathering places.

Ah, the smell of the marsh, the sounds of it all! A marsh wren titters close by. Endless streams of wavies move out to their morning meal, Canada grays come and go, local families organize for departure. An old mallard hen is talking from a muskrat lodge in her little cove. From over the lake comes the rollicking yodel of tundra swans just down from Keewatin, telling the whole wide world they have safely made another leg of their journey to Chesapeake and Currituck. The splash of a coot, the rustle of a red-winged blackbird bring peace for all who listen. Life began in the marshes, the ancients were sure of this. Then, now, and forevermore, life and mystery unfold behind a wall of reeds.

Such is the scene from my doorstep; the great marsh and its music reach to the horizon, wild and beautiful as when it belonged only to the native Cree, beyond compare this morning with skein after skein of lesser snow geese glaring white and dark above the autumn fields. They suffered hardships on their nesting grounds this year; the adults returning south lead only a few gray youngsters. But their numbers are secure. More than two million strong, they are one of the most plentiful wild geese in the world. Their eastern relative, the greater snow goose, had nearly vanished early in the century, declining below 3,000 birds. Now on the St. Lawrence River more than 300,000 are settled for a while before traveling on to the coasts of New Jersey, Delaware, and Maryland.

Only 30 years ago, the giant Canadas trading back and forth were considered extinct. In 1947, one old waterfowler declared that they were as scarce as flying saucers. Now, wonder of wonders, they grace our countryside in thousands, with a strong nesting population over much of the Lake Manitoba basin as well as in Minnesota and the Dakotas. The tundra swans (many more have passed by as I gather these thoughts) are thriving, adapting to a changing landscape. Once these new arrivals have rested, they will fly out to feed on harvested corn, a new crop on the northern prairie. After many rough years, the geese and swans are adapting to the environment we are modifying in so many ways.

Yes, we have helped by providing protection where it is lacking, sometimes "planting" populations by introducing preflight young to new places. Home is where a goose or swan takes its first flight. We give them only a start; they follow through, adapt, and multiply on their own. The raw nutrients wild geese leave on public lawns are nothing compared to the poisons mankind has added to the continent's lakes and rivers. Let us take the cue and accommodate as well.

Listen to those birds, watch them against the distant clouds. Great day in the morning, what a beautiful world this is! But there also is a prevailing sadness over this wide marsh. While geese and swans increase, ducks steadily decline. Each year fewer mallards and pintails, canvasbacks and redheads return from the wintering grounds; summer populations have thinned, and the autumn flights are reduced. This diminishment is not for Delta alone. The famous Big Grass

Marsh, many other of the so-called "duck factories" in Canada, and marshes great and small in Minnesota and the Dakotas have breeding populations below their potential. Even in dry years, too few ducks return to the nesting habitat that awaits them.

The scarcity of breeders in the spring flight is widely attributed to reproductive failures of the previous summer. Nesting is not only halted by the continuing drainage of wetlands; agriculture moves ever closer to the marsh's edge. This aggression against breeding habitat not only leaves ducks with fewer nesting coverts, but increases the success of foxes, raccoons, and other predators when they prey on eggs and nesting hens, especially in the critical early nesting period of April and May. Nesting ground losses add up to smaller fall flights and the inevitable reduction of birds returning to their breeding grounds in spring.

Problems with habitat degradation are only part of the story. Man himself is a major threat to ducks. In recent years, with fewer ducks in the fall flight, the kill by hunters did not decline. We have been taking more than nature provides. Beyond this, banding studies and bag tallies reveal a conspicuous "overharvest of hens" in years when breeding stocks are low.

Nine mallards swing into the wind, alighting in a little pond behind the reeds. These greenheads at my doorstep remind me that ducks are potentially the most manageable of all game birds. They lay large clutches. Most have nesting strongholds in middle latitudes, where they enjoy long nesting and rearing seasons. When first nests fail, they tend to try again. Breeders spread themselves widely over the prairie against the threat of local disasters. The mallard, one of the most important North American game birds, has many of the aggressive characteristics of such foreign interlopers as the English sparrow, starling, and ring-necked pheasant. Like these successful ruffians, it takes advantage of man's good nature wherever it can.

The pintail and blue-winged teal are exploitative, responding quickly to improvements in breeding environment. Like other game ducks, they adapt readily to man's presence. Canvasback and redhead often rear their broods within sight of farmhouse windows. Indeed, these and other prairie species nest within or at the edge of cities and towns where, as in metropolitan Minneapolis-St. Paul, and Regina, Saskatchewan, they have been more successful than on lakes and marshes beyond the city limits. The wild and wary black duck has bred in New York City's Central Park, and the wood duck, once close to extinction, nests widely in urban settings. By this evidence of close partnership with man, we know the wild duck's potential for reproduction if given the chance.

Predators are by no means absent from urban habitats. The main advantage appears to be higher survival of adult hens. These experienced mothers fledge their young early and are themselves strongly on the wing before they venture forth to meet gunfire. This is not said in praise of prairie cities, but simply to point out the lessons found there about the advantages of early production and the protection of mother ducks on the natal range.

The solution to the duck dilemma is imposing. It is our cue to adapt culturally—not simply for ducks, but in the long run, for ourselves. We must retreat a step or two from our intrusions upon the wild and natural edges of our world. We must follow the Mosaic Laws of animal husbandry in our annual waterfowl harvests. I have the hunch that we must take a more enlightened approach to the enjoyment and conservation of waterfowl, and that this book is a step in that direction. Here, as the birds seem to come alive before our eyes, we learn some of the simple details governing their lives. They will thrive if we allow them to follow their rules of life, and if we learn to share with them this world of land and water.

H. Albert Hochbaum

Delta, Manitoba
October 1987

Asquith Island, Maryland.

THE VOYAGE HOME

At winter's end, when the Arctic cold fronts sweeping over North America begin to weaken, waterfowl waiting out the season in the continent's milder latitudes grow restless. Soon, as spring weather patterns create strong southerly winds, flocks will begin voyages north to the marshes and tundra they regard as home, where the hens were hatched themselves, and where the older ones raised last year's young.

Some birds traverse the continent on their spring migrations, some shift only a few miles. Emperor geese winter on Alaskan shores, close to nesting ranges on the river deltas. Sizable flocks of giant Canada geese never go to Canada, nesting and wintering in Colorado, Missouri, and other western states, but most nest in the northern prairie states and neighboring Canadian provinces. Pushing against winter's southern limits, they sometimes arrive before the thaw, and must endure the year's last blizzard, nibbling crusty snow for want of drink. Often they are already nesting when robins return.

Arctic-nesting Ross' geese, white-fronted geese, black brant, tundra swans, and greater and lesser snow geese also travel just behind the thaw line. Though they are anxious to reach home, they often pause en route to fatten for the stresses of reproduction. Between northern farmlands and the still-frozen nesting ranges of the lesser snow goose, for example, lies Canada's forested Shield country, where vegetation thinly covers exposed bedrock and food is scarce.

They press on with May's favorable winds. Reaching the tundra at snow-melt, some start laying a day after arriving. Time is precious; the 11-week span from first egg to fledged gosling matches the length of the Arctic summer. Missing a few days of spring may put the brood in jeopardy at summer's end.

Fewer ducks than geese nest in the far north. Making their way in small flocks from wintering ranges in the Chesapeake Bay, the bottomlands of the Mississippi River, the Gulf coast, Mexico, and California, most travel toward nesting strongholds on the prairie marshes of the Dakotas, Manitoba, Saskatchewan, and Alberta. Here the last glaciers, retreating 10,000 years ago, left over ten million potholes, small, marshy ponds formed where the glaciers left massive ice fragments behind. Perhaps half of North America's game ducks nest on the prairies, including most mallards, pintails, blue-winged teal, shovelers, gadwalls, canvasbacks, redheads, and ruddy ducks. The black duck, whose numbers have declined continually since the 1940s, has traditionally nested throughout the eastern United States and Canada.

Struck by the precision with which waterfowl home to their natal wetlands each year after flying thousands of miles, many observers have looked to the earth's magnetic field or radio waves for explanations. Tantalizing as these possibilities are, a large body of evidence suggests that waterfowl *learn* their way to and from their birthplaces. Possessed of keen vision, migrating waterfowl clearly respond to the landforms beneath them; observers have seen flocks make turns of up to 45° as they come in sight of a river bend or a mountain. Perhaps they have also learned to guide themselves by the lights of cities and the swaths of superhighways.

Waterfowl are further guided in their flights by the stars, sun, and moon. They become disoriented on long journeys under heavy cloud cover, and in fog they are helpless, crash-landing anywhere—in trees, on highways, and against buildings. Storms can also down them; when migrating flocks get caught in bad weather, it is usually because they've traveled faster than the favorable weather that triggered the start of their flight. Intensely aware of air pressure and humidity, they prepare for long journeys hours before suitable conditions arrive, preening, flexing their wings, and foregoing shorter foraging flights. In spring, they take advantage of low pressure sys-

(Left) Lesser snow geese, near Westbourne, Manitoba.

(*Left*) Nesting pair attacking intruders.
(*Above*) At nest site, Lake Manitoba Marshes, Manitoba.

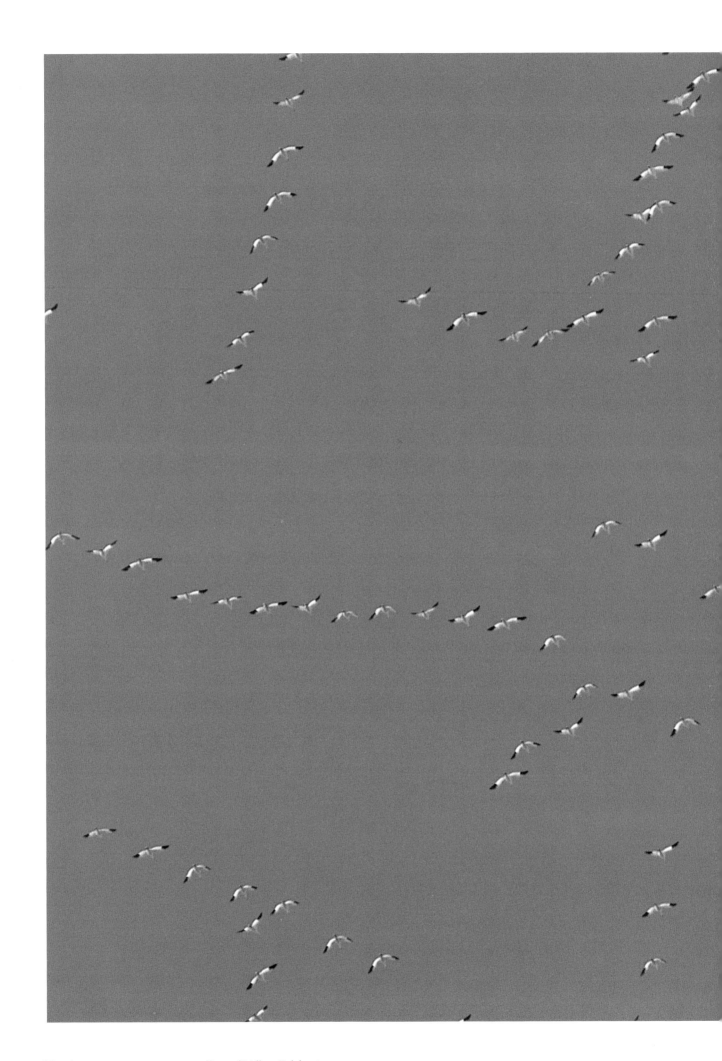

Snow geese and Ross' geese on spring migration, Central Valley, California.

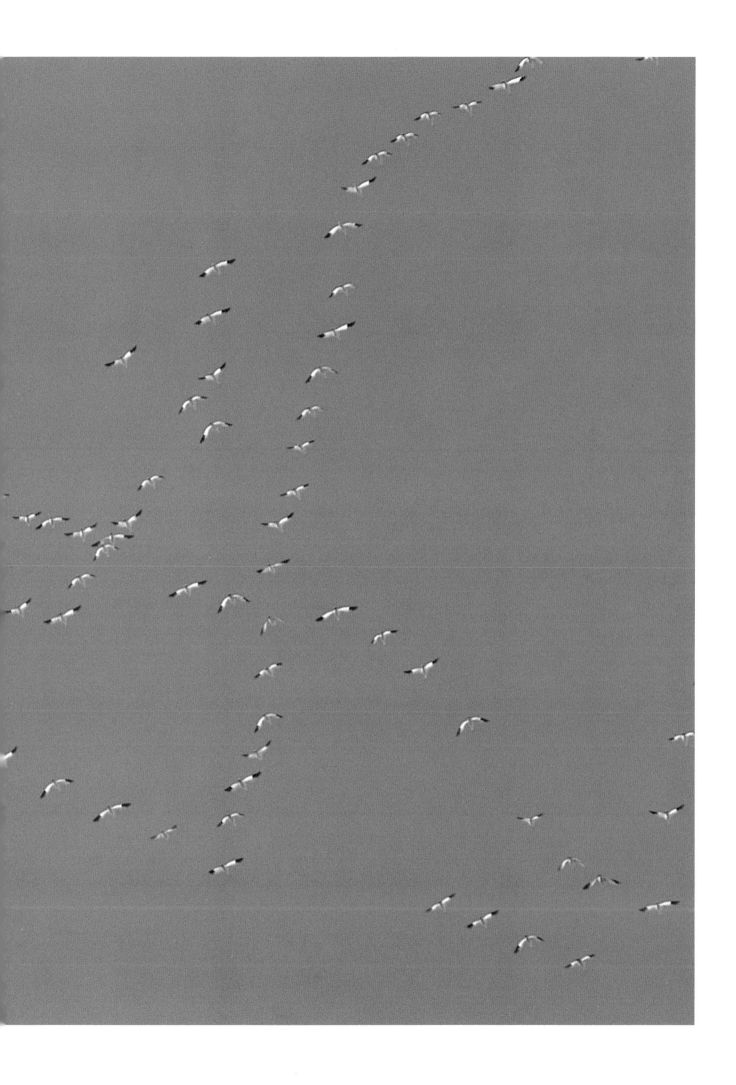

Mallard hen, Spirit Lake, Wisconsin.
(*Right*) Mallard drake speculum, Merced County, California.

(Left) Wood duck drake loafing, Allouez Bay, Wisconsin.
(Above) Preening his mate before copulation, Brule River, Wisconsin.

Common goldeneye hen leading courtship flight.

(Right) Migrational departure of common goldeneyes, Eau Claire River, Wisconsin.

(Left) Common goldeneye hen leading drake to nest site.
(Above) Courting goldeneye drakes performing "head-throw," Eau Claire River, Wisconsin.

Ring-necked duck pair on loafing spot, Allouez Bay, Wisconsin.

Redhead pairs on migrational stopover, Lake Manitoba Marshes, Manitoba.
(*Right*) Ruddy duck drake "rushing" in courtship, Bear River National Wildlife Refuge, Utah.

(Left) Lesser scaup drake joining courtship pursuit, Delta Marsh, Manitoba.
(Above) Unpaired lesser scaup hens and drakes, Spirit Lake, Wisconsin.

49

Blue-winged teal pair, Cape Cod, Massachusetts.

(*Left*) Early spring cattails, Everglades National Park, Florida.
(*Above*) Paired black-bellied whistling ducks, Aransas National Wildlife Refuge, Texas.

killed. When humans live nearby, she may fly under porches or farm machines or even alight at someone's feet. A pintail hen will tower toward the sun, then confound her pursuers by dropping abruptly from the zenith. Her aim is to rebuff these brutal gangs until she can be fertilized by a single drake for her renesting attempt.

Able to swim and walk shortly after hatching, ducklings follow their mother to food and water, quickly distinguishing her from all other ducks. At night and in storm, she continues to shelter them. Among early hatching dabbling ducks, she remains with her young until they can fly. Canvasbacks and redheads take longer to develop, and the hens usually abandon them before they fledge. Some of these young are not on the wing until mid-October, after hunting has started.

Drakes and hens molt separately, away from their young. Hens molt after abandoning their offspring in late summer. Mothers of late-hatched broods are still flightless during early hunting season. Drakes soon lose all sexual urges as they gather during May and June in ever-enlarging flocks of their own sex. They gravitate to traditional molting places, which may be far from the hens' breeding marshes. Mallards and other dabblers favor big marshes where there is plenty of cover and good food. Diving ducks go to shallow prairie lakes where open water offers safety and an abundance of sago pondweed and other aquatic plants.

Rapidly, drakes shed bright breeding dress and take on eclipse plumage, resembling hens' muted year-round appearance. This helps conceal them at the molt's peak, in July and August, when they cannot fly for three to four weeks. Once their wing and tail feathers grow in again, these late summer gatherings gradually disperse to new congregating areas. On waters from Alaska's Izembek Bay to Newfoundland's coast, waterfowl ready themselves for autumn's grand passages.

Pacific brant pair at nest, Yukon Delta, Alaska.

(*Left*) Pacific brant hen incubating.
(*Right*) Pacific brant hatchling, Yukon Delta, Alaska.

Cackling Canada goose and goslings, Yukon Delta, Alaska.

(Left) Tundra swan pair at nest. *(Above)* Trumpeter swan
parents leading three-day-old cygnets from threat, Henry's Lake, Idaho.

Month-old trumpeter cygnets, Yellowstone National Park, Wyoming.
(Right) Trumpeter pen and day-old cygnets, Henry's Lake, Idaho.

Mallard hen and two-week-old ducklings.
(Right) Sunning three-week-old mallard duckling, Spirit Lake, Wisconsin.

70

Mallard ducklings in tucked position for warmth, Spirit Lake, Wisconsin.
(Right) Mallard hen and brood, Allouez Bay, Wisconsin.

Wood duck hen leaving nest, Rich Hill, Missouri.

Day-old wood ducks preparing to tumble from nest, Rich Hill, Missouri.

THE SKIES OF AUTUMN

All summer, the sun's rays have warmed the broad, shallow lakes and bays of the north country, fostering a bounty of insects and plants. These waters, too open to serve breeding waterfowl, attract staging birds as days shorten and they seek fresh sources of food before migrating.

Drakes take wing for these wetlands after their new flight feathers grow. Fledgling ducks, left on their own, explore outward from their birthplaces, joining flocks of their kind wherever they find them. Only successful breeding hens, the last to molt, skulk flightless in reedy corners of their nesting marshes.

Nonbreeding Canada geese return from molting grounds to their clans on the nesting range, traveling sometimes from the Arctic to the prairies. In the Arctic, yearling snow geese also rejoin clans of their elders and the young of the year as these flocks move on to greater gatherings: 100,000 lesser snow geese fill the air with their commotion on the Mackenzie Delta, and 300,000 mass around the shores of James Bay.

These migrants feed intensely. At first, they move only short distances, until the young have built up strength for longer passages. Some, such as the Pacific brant on its way from Izembek Bay to Baja California, eventually travel for as long as 30 or 40 hours without stopping. Waterfowl which lack sufficient fat reserves to fly strongly throughout will be less likely to survive winter weather, predators, and sportsmen.

On prairie marshes, waterfowl depart in the same sequence each autumn. Blue-winged teal respond earliest, beginning to travel in August from Canadian breeding grounds to winter habitat in Mexico, the Caribbean, and Venezuela. Pintails fly through the west soon after, on their way to California's Central Valley, the Gulf coast, Mexico, and South America. Wigeons and shovelers go at September's end, gadwalls, ring-necked ducks, redheads, and canvasbacks in early October.

Lem and Steve Ward, decoy makers, Crisfield, Maryland.

Last to leave the north country, mallards, black ducks, goldeneyes, buffleheads, mergansers, and late contingents of scaups, tundra swans, and Canada geese wait until ice forms on the marshes, then hustle south on Arctic cold fronts in massive flights, flock after flock departing over the course of three or four days and soon dispersing across half the continent. In November 1947, at the peak of a three-day migrational surge, nearly 100,000 ducks crossed over Manitoba's Delta marsh in one hour, as equally huge flights traversed other Manitoba marshes. In subsequent days, watchers in eight midwestern states witnessed impressive segments of this same passage.

Most major fall migrations begin just after sundown under a clearing sky as an Arctic high-pressure system moves in. The barometer rises, the air grows colder and dryer, and the wind shifts to the northwest. As they travel, embedded within a mass of moving air, migrants' wing power sometimes pushes them into storms ahead of the system's leading edge. Though they often struggle through, they also are forced down to shelter on lakes and marshes, leading some observers to believe that storm, not clear weather, triggers migration.

The longer the journey, the higher the flight. Flocks of snow geese on their way from James Bay to Louisiana have interrupted commercial air travel in Canada. In contrast, sea ducks such as eiders and oldsquaws move south along the Atlantic and Pacific coasts only as far as they absolutely must. They travel a few yards above the water in flocks of a dozen or two, barreling down the troughs between ocean swells.

Autumn flights of waterfowl follow traditional corridors; banding studies show that they seek to rest at the same stopping places each autumn. Most of the continent's population of greater snow geese spends midautumn at Cap Tourmente on the St. Lawrence River below Quebec City, between Arctic nesting strongholds and mid-Atlantic coastal marshes. Lake Erie's Long Point is famed for the thousands of scaups, redheads, and canvasbacks which rest there. Many of the waterfowl wintering in the Pacific Flyway pause en route at Tule Lake and other wetlands in the Klamath Basin of Oregon and California.

Each year migrants face natural and manmade changes. Western waterfowl no longer gather in Utah's Bear River marshes, flooded in the mid-1980s by runoff from record snowfalls. On the lakes and rivers of North America's interior and in estuaries along both sea coasts, sewers, speedboats, and vacation homes poison and crowd out waterfowl. Traveling down the Mississippi Valley, waterfowl find fewer wetlands each autumn as they are lost to farming and flood control projects.

State and federal wildlife refuges save or replace some habitat. These refuges are funded by wildfowlers' fees and public taxes, and many serve as major public hunting areas. North America's 2.5 million waterfowlers, hunting on private and public land, annually harvest some 12 million ducks, 2.5 million geese, and several thousand tundra swans, an average of 6 ducks and 1 goose per hunter per year. In the "golden age" of late 19th-century hunting, bags of 50 and 100 birds a day were not unusual. The greatest market gunner of the early 20th century estimated that he killed half a million waterfowl in his lifetime, just a small part of the avalanche of ducks shipped to urban stores and restaurants in ice-filled railroad cars during the heyday of commercial hunting.

A number of states passed laws restricting waterfowl hunting during the 19th century, but federal regulations began with the signing of the Migratory Bird Treaty in 1916. Under this accord, the United States and Canada agreed to curtail market gunning, outlaw spring shooting, and protect the trumpeter swan, the wood duck, and the common eider, three species then near extinction.

Waterfowl numbers continued to dwindle in the 1920s, as severe droughts ravaged the Midwest and exploitation of wetlands quickened. The Roosevelt administration came up with a new source of funds for waterfowl conservation in 1934, the migratory bird hunting stamp. Together with funds from the Pittman-Robertson Act of 1937, which taxes arms and ammunition, the duck stamp has since brought in over a billion dollars for waterfowl management, and waterfowlers in the United States have borne much of the cost of protecting breeding and wintering habitats.

Private organizations have also helped; Ducks Unlimited, for example, has raised 400 million dollars in the last 50 years toward breeding habitat, and state groups like the Minnesota Waterfowl Association have grown strong recently. The Audubon Society, Nature Canada, the North American Wildlife Foundation, and many other wildlife organizations also contribute to waterfowl conservation with research and public education.

Despite all these efforts, the future of waterfowl in North America still isn't secure. Continuing declines among favored game species—mallards, pintails, black ducks, canvasbacks, and redheads—baffle waterfowl biologists. In the northern prairies there now appears to be more nesting habitat than waterfowl to nest there. In addition to questioning hunter harvests, wildlife managers and biologists have considered the increasing vulnerability of nesting ducks to predators and the subtle effects of "invisible" pollutants such as acid rain, which reduce essential food supplies in the water without leaving obvious marks of damage.

While concern mounts over causes and solutions for declines in game duck populations, wildfowling traditions, from decoy making to training retrievers, carry on. Unwary by nature, waterfowl learn caution if they survive early encounters with hunters, and their wings speedily carry them out of range when

McGeorge's Reservoir, near Pine Bluff, Arkansas.

they sense ⟨
techniques,
were outlaw⟨
the carved ⟨
main ploys.

A wall-pa⟨
him hunting
of the Nile 4,
goes back at l⟨
coy" comes fr⟨
trap, the "en⟨
wild birds to
ners borrowe⟨
to their guns.

North Ame⟨
Indians, who s⟨
or fashioned
Colonists beg⟨
century. Betw⟨
when deman⟨
developed dis⟨
large numbers
made large an⟨
where eiders a⟨
gave mallard a⟨
for floating in r⟨
painting. Loui⟨
species rarely ⟨
and ring-necke⟨

Specially bre⟨
wildfowlers' es⟨
hunters develop
trained to inter⟨
prancing on the⟨
Chesapeake Bay⟨
with gentle mou⟨
dor retrievers, t⟨
hardly a suburb⟨
black labs and g⟨
the art of wildfo⟨

Canada geese going out to feed, Horicon National Wildlife Refuge, Wisconsin.
(Right) Wildfowler calling mallards, Rio Grande Valley, New Mexico.

(*Left*) Cottonwood. (*Above*) Shovelers near migration's end,
Bosque del Apache National Wildlife Refuge, New Mexico.

Pintails, American wigeon, green-winged teal, and mallards
startled by gunshot, Merced National Wildlife Refuge, California.

Preening trumpeter cygnets, Yellowstone National Park, Wyoming.
(Right) Lesser snow geese, Bosque del Apache National Wildlife Refuge, New Mexico.

WINTERING HAVENS

Traditional ice-free havens where North American waterfowl settle in for the winter have legendary names among sportsmen and birdwatchers: Barnegat and Chesapeake Bay, Currituck Sound and the Santee River in the east; Puget Sound, Scammon's Lagoon, San Francisco Bay, and Bosque del Apache in the west. Coastal ranges of wintering waterfowl reach from Nova Scotia to the Gulf of Mexico, and from the Aleutians to South America. Inland, the hardwood swamps of the lower Mississippi River and the lakes and rivers of the Rockies' Great Basin also receive the traveling flocks.

The moment they touch down, swans, geese, and ducks begin seeking food to recover from the journey south, to survive winter, and to build up vigor for courting, pairing, and returning to the north country. In December, restored to the full brilliance of their courting plumage, drakes are ready for the huge winter meetings of young and old, male and female, where they compete for mates.

Now, too, different species meet, sharing open water and marshland. Mallards, pintails, gadwalls, and other dabblers sometimes feed in mixed flocks. The wigeon has long been noted for its habit of snooping about the edges of feeding rafts of canvasbacks and redheads, waiting until these divers come up with succulent strands of underwater plants, then snatching them away. Most species, however, stay with their own kind. From miles across the water, Chesapeake Bay watermen can tell the flocks apart: redheads feeding and loafing in tight, even-edged rafts, canvasbacks rafting in looser, rough-edged groups, and lesser scaup strung out in ragged assemblies.

As they feed, different species share some areas, but each favors a distinct niche in the range from open sea to freshwater pond. Eiders, oldsquaws, and other sea ducks thrive on the ocean, where

Canvasbacks feeding in observation tank, Lacrosse, Wisconsin.

they make deep dives for the mollusks and crustaceans they prefer. Cruising near outcrops in surging seas, harlequin ducks ride swells to snatch at mollusks hanging from the rocks' seaweed mane.

Atlantic and Pacific brant depend heavily on eelgrass, which grows in shallow tidal zones along both coasts. They suffered sharp population losses during a widespread eelgrass blight in the 1930s. Brant and emperor geese mainly eat the leaves, but the growth of this underwater plant shelters countless creatures, including crabs, mollusks, and insect larvae—food for scaup and scoter.

Canvasbacks, redheads, and other prairie-bred diving ducks, physically adapted to spending most of their time in the water, gather in brackish sounds, estuaries, and wide river mouths, where they find wild celery, wigeon grass, and sago pondweed. Like eelgrass, these underwater plants harbor plenty of small animal life. The canvasback's long, narrow bill is suited to digging out aquatic tubers and rootstalks. *Aythya valisineria,* the canvasback's scientific name, honors its love of wild celery, *Vallisineria spiralis,* although ornithologists and botanists disagree on the spelling.

The canvasback's close relatives, redhead and scaup, have wider bills, adapted to a more varied diet. The shoveler, equipped with a large, trowel-shaped bill lined with small, toothlike projections called *lamellae,* shovels in and strains large quantities of plankton.

Pintails and other dabbling ducks haunt the water's shallow edges, where logs, sandbars, and muskrat houses provide the solid resting places they require. Tipping up to feed, they stretch their necks toward plants and crustaceans. In the past 50 years, mallards and pintails have grown increasingly fond of feeding on cereal grains in farmers' fields—corn near the Chesapeake Bay, and rice in Louisiana, Texas, and California.

Geese, too, have shifted from marshes and wild lands to farming country. Attracted by waste corn in Maryland and Virginia, Canada geese have become a major winter presence on the Chesapeake Bay. Tundra swans have followed them into the fields, as have lesser snow geese. Greater snow geese in the east still favor brackish and saltwater flats where they find the rootstalks of sedges.

Waterfowl seldom pass the entire winter in one neighborhood. Wind and weather prompt daily shifts to protected spots. Flocks fly around on fine days, keeping their flying muscles fit. Food supplies diminish, or the changing season may trigger a change in diet. As spring approaches, female ducks turn from aquatic plants, rich in carbohydrates, to larvae and crustaceans, loaded with protein.

Flocks travel away from bad weather; when the upper Chesapeake Bay freezes, diving ducks withdraw to Currituck Sound in North Carolina. Extreme cold doesn't always prompt travel. Canvasbacks and black ducks have perished in severe winters on New York's Finger Lakes, lacking incentive to fly further south.

Human disturbances also unsettle waterfowl, driving them from food and safe water. It may seem like a momentary fright when a passing motorboat startles birds into the air, but ever-increasing numbers of motorboats in many recreational waters have harried flocks enough that they abandon them altogether, even if food and shelter are plentiful. Heavy shoreline activities probably contributed to the major shift of wintering Pacific brant from the coast of Washington, Oregon, and California to the bays of Baja California.

Just as waterfowl have lost migrational stopping places in autumn, they have lost significant habitat throughout the country. In the 1920s, flocks of canvasback on the Chesapeake Bay's Susquchanna Flats rose "like smoke" when they took wing. But pollu-

Spectacled eider, Sea World, San Diego, California.

tion and heavy silt loads from upstream on the Susquehanna River have wiped out the Flats' wild celery beds. Populations of canvasback in the Chesapeake are sadly diminished now, and to survive, they feed on crustaceans, a diet which has spoiled their sweet flavor for hunters. Waterfowl biologists, troubled by the species' continuing decline, also ask whether the change in diet has lessened their ability to endure winter with strength for the breeding season.

No wintering ranges have suffered greater losses than California's Central Valley and the sloughs and hardwood swamps of the lower Mississippi River. Ninety-five percent of the Central Valley's precolonial wetlands have disappeared. Food and water on what remains continue to draw wintering flocks, but to keep fit and socialize, waterfowl also need wide spaces. Crowding of flocks on these winter ranges intensifies the destructive power of pollution from agricultural run-off and of botulism and other avian plagues.

Hunting also follows waterfowl south on their wintering ranges. Hunting seasons are staggered latitudinally, roughly matching the southward flow of waterfowl; as hunting ends in a northern zone, many ducks have moved on to a new hunting season further south. Some geese and ducks feel hunting pressure from September 1, when they leave Arctic and boreal nesting ranges, to late January at their wintering marshes on the lower Mississippi and the Gulf coast.

In good years, when waterfowl bring many fledglings south from nesting ranges, the birds of the year make up most of the kill, not only because they outnumber adults, but because, as studies have shown, they learn about decoys and hunters slowly. The predominance of youngsters in good years buffers the warier adults, but when summer has been hard and young are scarce, adult losses mount.

Bandings and other life studies show that despite

their potential life span of up to 20 years, few female game ducks live beyond their third summer. Years of experience give a hen more strategies for outwitting predators and becoming a successful breeder. When adults dominate a waterfowl population year after year, a cumulative pattern of success is set in motion: adults form their pairs earlier, reach the breeding grounds sooner, and bring off their broods more rapidly than young birds, allowing both themselves and their broods more time on the wing before the stresses of migration. Protection from hunters during their delayed flightless period gives adult hens a greater chance of living through the year and repeating the successful cycle.

In midwinter, when large populations have assembled, we see the make-up of waterfowl populations clearly: the firm pair bonds and distinct family groups of geese and swans, and the ratios of male to female ducks. Among many duck species there is a growing imbalance in favor of males. Canvasback drakes now outnumber hens by seven to three, and similar figures hold true for redhead and lesser scaup. Under these circumstances, there can only be 30,000 pairs for every 100,000 canvasbacks. Recent winter counts of mallards and pintails suggest that the imbalance between the sexes is growing for these species too.

Toward winter's end, increasing daylight and advancing spring weather alert waterfowl to the journey ahead and intensify courtship among unpaired drakes and hens. Pintails and canvasbacks shoot through the air in chase groups. Wood ducks, preening in ritual patterns, display their bright feathers to the hens. Goldeneyes and buffleheads enact the rapid, machinelike motions of their courting rites. As winds shift, the thawline moves north over the continent, and the travelers—some paired, some still courting as they travel, geese and swans bound in family groups—begin their voyage home.

Adult and young lesser snow geese, Tule Lake National Wildlife Refuge, California.

Trumpeter swans on winter fly-around, Red Rocks Lake National Wildlife Refuge, Montana.

(*Left*) Trumpeter swan, Minnesota.
(*Above*) Unpaired yearling tundra swans, Choptank River, Maryland.

(Left) Canada geese in family groups, Grantsburg, Wisconsin.
(Above) Delta Marsh, Manitoba.

Canada geese, Tule Lake National Wildlife Refuge, California.

Lesser snow geese, Ross' geese, and sandhill cranes, Bosque del Apache
National Wildlife Refuge, New Mexico.

126

Snow geese, Lake Ocheda, Minnesota.

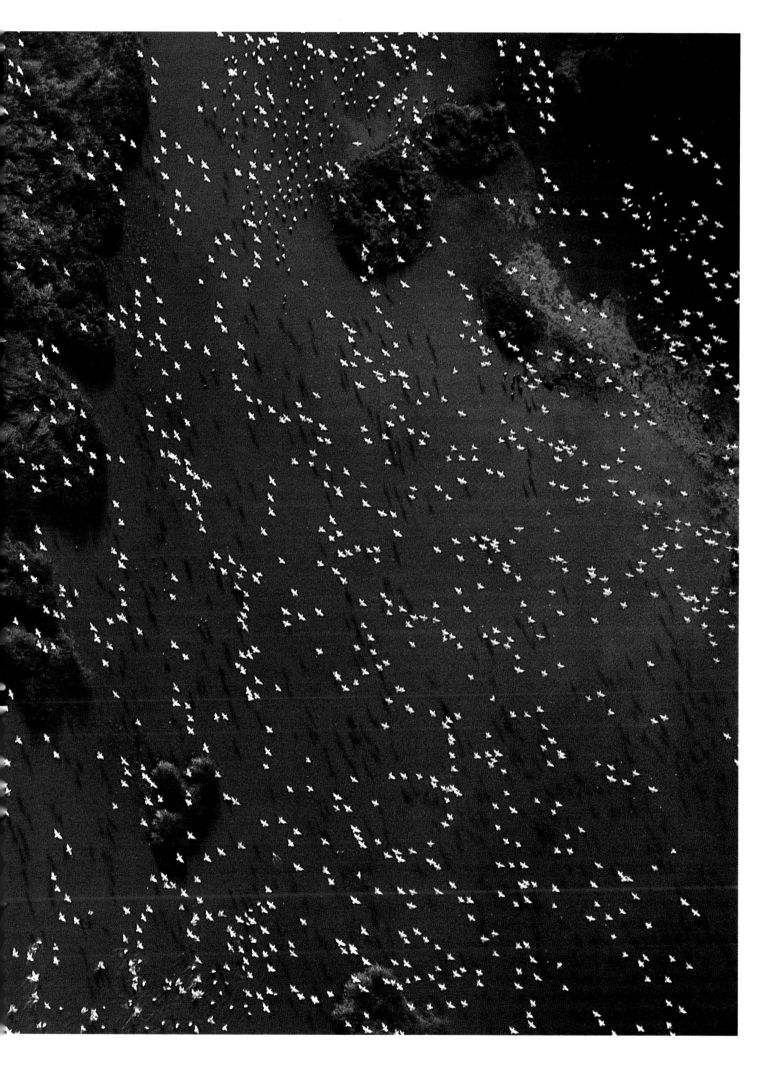

129

Tundra swans, Swanquarter, North Carolina.

Cattail pond, Minnedosa, Manitoba.
(Right) Canvasback pair, Lake Andes National Wildlife Refuge, South Dakota.

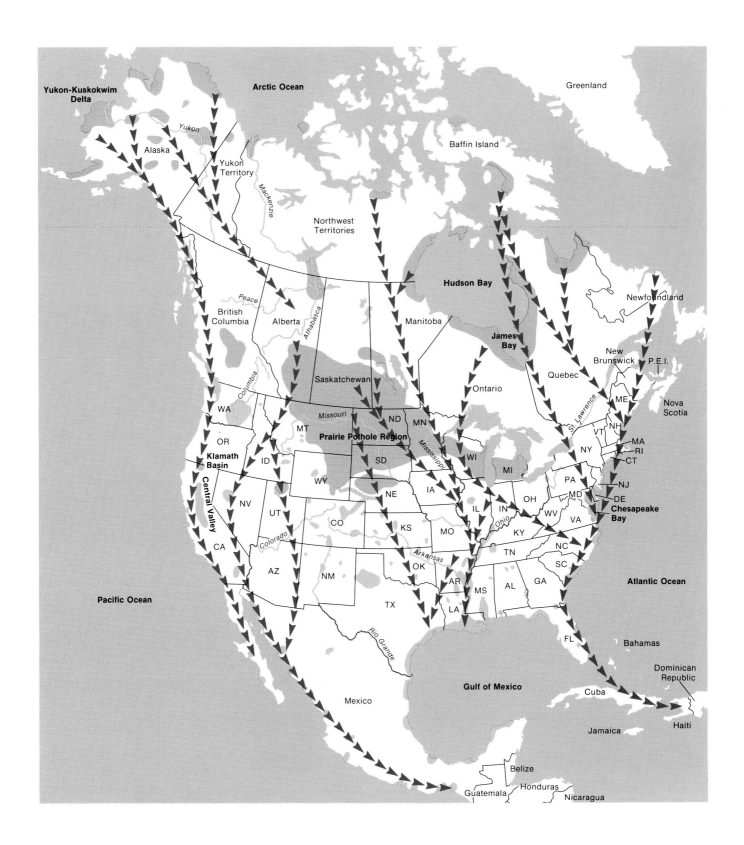

North American Waterfowl Migration

▨ **Important Breeding Areas**

▨ **Important Wintering Areas**

▼ **Fall Migration Corridors**

Photography Credits

Sam Abell: pages 84-85. **Jack A. Barrie:** cover, pages 23, 24 (lower), 24-25, 43 (right), 44-45, 48, 86-87, 98 (left), 98-99, 119 (right), 124 (left), and 124-125. **Gary Braasch:** pages 92-93. **Matt Bradley:** pages 82-83. **Jim Brandenburg:** pages 2-3, 54-55, 90-91, 106, 114 (lower), 120-121, and 128-129. **Glenn D. Chambers:** pages 51 (lower), 55 (right), 74, 75, 77, and 78. **Glenn D. Chambers/Ducks Unlimited, Inc.:** pages 18, 50-51, 62, 66 (lower), and 130-131. **DRK/Photo:** pages 52-53. **Skylar Hansen:** pages 66-67, 68 (left), 68-69, 104 (left), 112-113, and 116-117. **Steve Kaufman:** pages 47 (lower), 57, 60-61, 63, and 64-65. **Yogi Kaufman:** pages 8, 16-17, 35, 38 (left), 46-47, 79, 95, 97, 104-105, 122 (left), and 136. **Frans Lanting:** pages 110-111. **Bates Littlehales:** pages 45 (lower), 76, 80, 102 (lower), 102-103, 108-109, 122-123, and 126-127. **Scott Nielsen:** pages 4-5, 6-7, 11, 12, 28-29, 30 (left), 30-31, 32-33, 33 (lower), 34-35, 35 (lower), 36-37, 40-41, 42-43, 49, 70-71, 71 (left), 72 (left), 72-73, 94, 118-119, and back cover. **Jerome R. Serie:** pages 132-133. **Connie Toops:** page 56. **Glen Van Nimwegen:** pages 38-39 and 88-89. **L. B. Wales:** pages 114-115. **Gary Zahm:** pages 10, 20-21, 26-27, 29 (right), 89 (right), 93 (right), 96, 100-101, and 133 (lower).

For Further Reading

Bellrose, Frank C. *Ducks, Geese & Swans of North America.* Harrisburg, Pennsylvania: Stackpole Books, 1976.

Delacour, Jean. *The Waterfowl of the World.* 4 vols. London: Country Life, Ltd., 1954-1964.

Elman, Richard. *The Atlantic Flyway.* Photography by Walter Osborne. Tulsa, Oklahoma: Winchester Books, 1980.

Hanson, H. C. *The Giant Canada Goose.* Carbondale: Southern Illinois University Press, 1965.

Hochbaum, H. Albert. *The Canvasback on a Prairie Marsh.* Washington, D.C.: American Wildlife Institute, 1944.

Hochbaum, H. Albert. *Travels and Traditions of Waterfowl.* Minneapolis: University of Minnesota Press, 1955.

Johnsgard, Paul A. *Waterfowl of North America.* Bloomington and London: Indiana University Press, 1975.

Phillips, J. C. *The Natural History of the Ducks.* 4 vols. Boston: Houghton Mifflin, 1923-1926.

Walsh, Harry M. *The Outlaw Gunner.* Cambridge, Maryland: Tidewater Publishers, 1971.

Emperor goose hen on nest, Yukon Delta, Alaska.